C000101196

A LOVE SO STRONG

The highs and lows of early motherhood

BY MARIA TEMPANY

Acknowledgements

Cover Illustrations by Nicole Wegman @art_to_remember_by_nw
All Poetry Copyright

ISBN: 978-1-7398360-0-9
Year of Publication: 2021

Book Design: Rachel Dickens @lollysnow

Illustrations by:
Page 18, 35 & 63: Claudia Adro @theartofcadro
Page 23, 51 & 59: Chloe Trayhurn @chloe_trayhurn_art
Page 29, 37 & 77: Alice Atkinson @alice_atkinson_illustration
Page 32, 45, 49, 73, 91, 92 & 95: Nicole Wegman
Page 41: Jojo Ford @jojofordillustration
Page 52, 57 & 86: Carole-Anne Brugere @charlie_mamas
Page 56 & 72: Rachel Dickens @lollysnow
Page 64 & 89: Lisa Fama www.handdrawnbylisa.com
Page 81: Natasha Moon @oakpea.design
Page 85: Sophie Ficek @sophsscrawls

2022

To my dearest Annie,

I hope this book warms your heart the way it does mine, when you look at your precious sons growing and thriving.. You are the best Mummy in the world to your boys. It's so lovely to watch you together, such a strong bond, "A love so strong". Enjoy all the little poems that help put into words the overwhelming love you have for them.

Love you forever & always,

Sazzy xxxxx
& Conor xxxxx

Words of Praise for Maria's Work

"She has a talent for expressing the words
you can't find yourself."

"Her words have helped me feel less
alone waking up in the morning.
It means so much that others are feeling the struggle too."

"All her work is so relatable and realistic. It somehow makes
me cherish the love I have for my newborn a little more."

"I wish I had this when my babies had
me up all night. So meaningful."

"I love poetry but never came across anything
like this. So unique and special."

"So comforting to read. Better than any
chocolates at three in the morning!"

"Truly an amazing writer: Heart-warming and kind."

" A beautiful heart-warming book filled
with a bundle of emotions, a true reflection
of the journey that is motherhood."

NOTE FROM THE AUTHOR

Thank you for supporting this
passion project of mine.
Nothing could have prepared me for
the whirlwind of becoming a mother:
the exhaustion, the doubt, the guilt,
the fear, but most of all, the love:
that overwhelming, all-consuming love:
terrifying and exhilarating all at once.
These poems have been an outlet and a safe
space for me to voice the highs and lows of my
early mothering days thus far. My aim is that
they might offer comfort and solace to mums all
over and reassure them that they are not alone.

With love and best wishes,
Maria Tempany

A love so strong, a love so wide,
a love so deep that's sure to guide
You onwards when you lose your way.
When all else fails, that love will stay.

So, don't forget, when next you fear
which path to take: The answer's clear.
Look within and trust your heart.
That love will show you where to start.

CONTENTS

BLISSFUL MOMENTS

All I wish for you

YOURS

For only a short time
Are you truly all mine.
But, for all of my lifetime,
Will I be ever thine.

MY WISHES FOR YOU

I want you to feel.
I want you to dream.
I want you to love
'til you burst at the seams.

I want you to hurt,
Strange though that may sound,
For in hurting we grow
And a new strength is found.

I want you to always
Stay true to yourself.
I pray that you will always
Stay in good health.

I wish that in every day
You will find joy.
I hope you'll be happy
My sweet little boy.

UNWAVERING LOVE

I will forever hold you
in my arms, then in my heart,
For this unwavering love
will travel anywhere you art.

I'm sure some day you'll venture
places my hands cannot reach
But do not fear, I'll be right here:
I long so much to teach

you strength and self-belief,
courage and humility.
I pray you'll always emanate
the joy you bring to me.

So, if sometimesyou wonder
why I hold you very close.
I want you to always be safe:
This I wish for the most.

I LOVE YOU, MAMA

There are so many moments
I try desperately to clutch,
Like when you turn to me and say:
"I love you very much."

I want to bottle up those words,
and YOU, just as you are.
And yet, of course, I want your wings
to help you venture far.

It's divine and yet conflicted,
this whirlwind of emotion.
You evoke in me the strongest sense
of pure and raw devotion.

While, of course the tantrums challenge me,
each and every day.
They quickly are forgotten
when you turn to me and say:

"I love you, Mama: very much."
And, in those words, I melt.
In all the world, I don't believe,
a greater love was felt.

HOME TO MUM

Long may these magical
moments last.
I sure will be sad
when all these days have passed.

Venture onwards my babies
and you'll conquer all.
Enjoy each new adventure
no matter how small.

Love Fiercely. Fall hard.
Be courageous and strong.
Follow your heart
and it won't lead you wrong.

And on the days
when you're feeling all glum,
My arms will be open.
Come home here to mum.

A Love So Strong

JUGGLING IT ALL

Energy waning,
but a heart never so full

A DREAM COME TRUE

"What a gorgeous baby!
He must be a dream come true?"
Please don't forget to say to mum:
"He's great, but how are YOU?"

This precious new arrival
will have brought much disarray.
So, make sure you inquire:
"Can I help in any way?"

"He's perfect, but I'm struggling."
A tale as old as time.
These overwhelming feelings
are a challenge to define.

"Every inch of me is aching.
I've been truly torn apart.
It's hard to grasp this newfound love
consuming all my heart."

Tiny steps, my dear old friend,
for baby and YOU too.
This world is new for baby,
but it's also new for you.

Give yourself some time, my love.
Just take it day by day.
You're growing too. You'll find your feet.
The pain WILL go away.

And, when you think you've grasped it:
This mothering, I mean.
Another hurdle will appear
to rip you at the seams.

You'll stumble all along the way,
but falter you will not.
You'll never cease to be amazed
by the strength that you've now got.

And on those days that push you
to the depths of much despair.
Look right into their little eyes
and you'll find comfort there.

Nothing could prepare us
for this ocean of unknown.
Please always know,
no matter what,
that you are not alone.

WHO HOLDS MUM?

Everyone wants the baby
To pass amongst each other.
But who holds the woman
who's just become mother?

there is
hope
there is
light
alice
atkinson

THE CAUSE WILL BE THE CURE

Today there was nothing
that I could do right.
Everything was a struggle.
It was fight after fight.

There was many a tear
And tantrums a plenty.
My energy tank
Was running on empty.

She wouldn't sleep
and he wouldn't eat.
By lunch I resigned
to admitting defeat.

Time for the tv
and cuddles galore.
Patience wearing thin and
I can't take much more!

When right in that moment
As I needed it most,
You gazed up at me
And snuggled in close.

In that one precious moment
Of redeeming grace.
I found the solace I sought,
In the smile on your face.

So, when you start to question
If this you can endure.
You can and you will:
The cause will be the cure.

They don't mean to push us
And make it so tough
And they hold healing power
On the days the most rough.

So, please this do remember,
When you struggle to cope:
They'll guide us through. Of this I'm sure:
Please never give up hope.

Maria Tempany @therhymingone

MAGIC IN THE MAKING

Nothing ever rattled me
Quite like motherhood:
The land that's filled with doubt and fear
And 'what if' or 'I should'.

We question ourselves daily.
A mother's guilt is real.
Most days we can't explain the role
And how it makes us feel.

We're fulfilled yet often empty,
Never still and craving space
To sit and be and take it in:
To find our perfect pace.

And yet there's something in it,
In motherhood, I mean:
A magic in the making,
Invisible, yet seen

Each day in all those little smiles
And in each loving glance.
From the moment that we met, my heart:
It didn't stand a chance.

So, though rattled that I really am,
I'll keep on muddling through,
For there is no greater power
Than the love I have for you.

THOSE UNSPOKEN WORDS

I don't want to snap
and I don't want to fight.
I want everything
to just be 'alright'.

But, these sure are waters
never waded before,
And I know that it's not
our intention to war.

Yet, that is quite often
the way that it seems
as we struggle to hear
above all of their screams

the unspoken words
that we're shouting inside.
When I said I was fine,
I'm sorry. I lied.

I guess what I meant
was that I really miss
the way that WE were
before, well, all of this:

This chaos, this whirlwind,
this turbulent time.
Each day is survival.
There's no space that's mine.

It's all about them,
as it should be in ways,
but it was US before them,
and I miss that some days.

So, when I snap at you
to 'get this' or 'go there'.
Be patient with me,
and please know that I care

about them, about us,
more than you'll ever know,
But some days I struggle
To let that love show.

ACHING ARMS

I know your arms are aching and your back is under strain.
I assure you that your struggles and these aches are not in vain.

The days will soon get brighter.
The load you carry will get lighter.

But, that love that guides you onwards will not wane.

may my arms
forever
be your place
of safety

WORDS OF ENCOURAGEMENT

A Reminder on Those Tougher Days

YOU'RE DOING GREAT

Hello Mama!
You're doing great.
It WILL get better:
Just you wait.

It's hard to picture
that right now,
But this fog WILL lift:
This I do vow.

You're everything
they need and more
no matter what,
And they adore

Your smell, your touch,
Your every being.
There's nothing that
can stop them seeing

All the love
You radiate.
You've got this mum:
You're doing great.

You're doing great

THE BIRTH OF A MOTHER

They say with the birth
of each babe also comes
the birth of a mother,
and no doubt all you mums

Will nod and agree that,
though weary and worn,
When our babies arrive
A new, fierce love is born.

Priorities shift
In the blink of an eye.
The world has new meaning:
They're your sea and your sky.

In trying so hard
To keep them alive,
We can often struggle
To barely survive.

But, little by little,
We fill our new shoes:
Euphoric moments
Amongst those baby blues.

The love that consumes us
Is second to none
And we grow every day
On this journey as mum.

GOOD ENOUGH

Every evening as I lay
my babies down to rest
I find myself reflecting
if I did my very best.

Did I shout too much today?
Say "No" too frequently?
I'm sorry If I haven't laughed
or played much recently.

I'm really very tired
and some days it is quite tough.
I cannot keep from wondering
if I am good enough.

Meanwhile, in their little minds,
as they drift off to sleep,
A different narrative takes hold
as they sail towards slumbers deep.

"My Mama means to world to me.
She sees my every need.
She always knows just what to do.
She's safety guaranteed.

When I feel a little sad,
I reach to hold her hand
and then I'm cured. She is, for sure,
the best mum in this land!"

So, please remember, all you mums,
that when this road is rough:
You ARE the perfect mum for them.
You're more than good enough.

I SEE YOU

I see you mum as you sit there
With tired eyes and messy hair.

I see you mum. Don't try to hide
The struggles that you face inside.

I see you mum. I really do.
I see the toll this takes on you.

Each day is filled with fret and fears.
Always on the brink of tears.

I see you mum. In you I see:
Every. Aching. Part of me.

But, mum, there's something else I see:
A strength that's oh so clear to me.

You may not feel it through the haze,
The struggles and the tiresome days

But you are perfect, as you are.
Your love for them will guide you far.

And you'll look back on days like these
With so much love. Hang in there. Please.

A Love So Strong

FINDING OUR VOICE

The realisation that no-one has it all figured out and trusting our instinct

DANGER NAP

Today we had a 'danger' nap:
Asleep at four o'clock.
Despite what all the books may say,
We didn't die of shock.

We snuggled in and basked in it:
That rare moment of calm.
I wondered how this could be 'dangerous'
As I stroked your tiny palm.

Some respite in a busy day
And much comfort indeed.
A 'danger' nap, it seems to me,
Was what we both did need.

"She'll never sleep tonight",
Or "You'll pay for that", 'they' say.
But, for this moment here,
it is a price I'll gladly pay.

For contact, 'danger' naps
Are precious moments to behold,
And I promise you what 'they' say,
matters not if truth be told.

A Love So Strong

MOTHER

M(ama's marvellous milk, filled with
goodness and warmth for an)other

A MOTHER'S WORTH

The nature of their baby's birth
Does not define a mother's worth.

A Love So Strong

Maria Tempany @therhymingone

FEED TO SLEEP

"You've got to be kidding!
You still feed her to sleep?"
Did I seek your opinion?
And, if not, you can keep

all your thoughts and your views
about how I should raise
MY babies inside and, perhaps,
you might praise

me for doing my best.
For following my heart.
As this mothering business
is a whirlwind, an art.

A series of tests,
Challenges and trials,
But daily rewarded
by their precious smiles.

We're all doing our best.
My road differs from thine.
So, follow YOUR gut
and let me follow mine.

SLEEPLESS NIGHTS

The Permanent Exhaustion

Maria Tempany @therhymingone

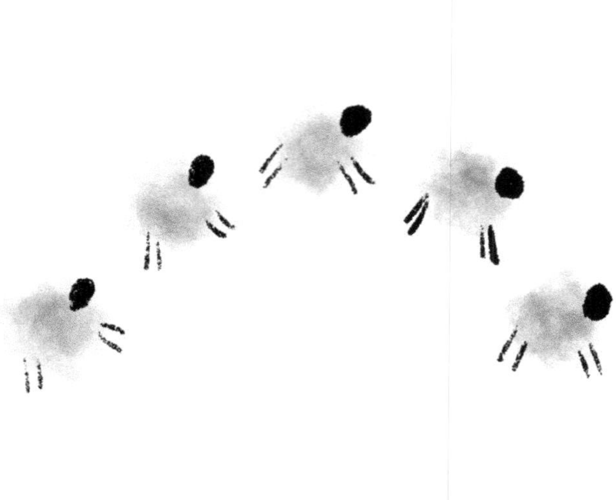

COUNTING SHEEP

I frequently wonder if I will again sleep
that restorative kind of slumber, so deep:

Where you're out like a light
At the start of the night

And not sitting up counting sheep.

RESOLUTION

Reso(lved to the fact
That we're a sleepless institution.
Acceptance is, without doubt,
The only so)lution.

YOU ARE NOT ALONE

For all those who are struggling:
Please know that you are seen.
You do not walk this path alone,
lonely though it may seem.

As you pace the floors at night
or rock your babe to sleep,
Parents all across the globe
your company do keep.

When tears fall from your tired eyes
and you can't see the light,
I promise you that someone else
is fighting that same fight.

Yes, it's true, the years fly by,
but all those nights are long.
And just because you struggle,
doesn't mean that you're not strong.

For, in fact, each day you're showing
strength you never knew you had,
And I promise you that all the good days
WILL outweigh the bad.

So, hang in there, you're doing great
and you are not alone.
You'll be guided by the greatest love
That you have ever known.

A Love So Strong

TIME FLYING BY

Snippets of emerging independence and vibrant personalities

THAT FLASH OF INDEPENDENCE

A single tear slid down my cheek
As we said goodbye today,
As right before that moment,
You did turn to me and say:

"See you later, mama.
My friends are waiting here."
So confident and happy:
Not a worry, nor a fear.

A flash of independence
that took me by surprise.
You already need me less
and so the tears filled up my eyes.

I fought them back and said: "Have fun,"
As you ran through the door.
With every passing day, my dear,
I love you more and more.

CADRO

FIERCE

Ferocious fire in your soul.
Innocence that radiates.
Energy in bounds and bounds.
Resounding cheer you emanate.
Call you fierce? I'm sure they may.
Ever enchanting, I pray you'll stay.

MISCHIEF

I stumbled on this moment
amidst the chaos of the day.
A moment that, though time will pass,
with me will always stay.

Your sister slipped and hit her head.
My goodness did she yell.
So, off you flew, right to her side,
and banged your head as well.

That glint of mischief in your eyes,
stopped in hers the falling tears.
Your instinct knew to soothe her
despite your paucity of years.

Then, you laughed together.
Yes, you chased her pain away.
What a magic moving moment
That with me will always stay.

OUR BABY, NOW A BOY

It's like it happened overnight:
Our baby, now a boy.
A little man who fills this house
With innocence and joy.

I marvel at it really.
Where did the time go?
Those early days felt endless
Now, each time I blink, you grow.

Of course it has to happen.
This I do understand.
But each milestone seems to hit me
Much harder than I'd planned.

Barely walking, next you're running.
Oh, to slow the wheels of time.
Barely words, next detailed phrases,
From this little boy of mine.

'They' say: "Soak it up. It goes so fast."
And this is surely true.
So, I'll savour every moment
Of each day I have with you

CHRISTMAS EVE

Tonight we spent the evening
with two babies on our hips.
I could not have conjured up
a better Christmas Eve than this.

So content amidst the chaos
with no fear of missing out,
For these perfect bundles in our arms
are what it's all about.

"Will I get to see Santa?"
You'll be fast asleep my dear,
But in your dreams this evening
In his sleigh he will appear.

And if you hear some noises:
Please don't get a fright.
His reindeer's hooves will settle
on your roof deep in the night.

And when you wake tomorrow morn
and wipe those sleepy eyes,
For you, beneath the Christmas Tree,
will wait a nice surprise.

For, without a doubt, my babies,
You've been very good this year.
Despite the tough times we've been through,
You've filled us with good cheer.

CHANGING BODIES

The Ever-Persistent Battle with Body Image

I'VE REALLY LET MYSELF GO

"I've really let myself go."
A statement so often heard.
Words drenched with deep meaning
That should really be shared.

Gone where? To do what?
It's quite frankly absurd.
Yet, in that simple statement,
So much angst is inferred.

We're tired. We're weary.
Our self-worth has waned.
Our confidence shattered:
Our waistbands are strained.

These beautiful babies
Demand all our attention.
A love so consuming:
A love too great to mention.

What if, to our bodies,
Some of that love was shown?
What if we marvelled
At the miracles we've grown.

Body parts one time firm,
Are now soft, but so strong.
Perhaps that is how
they were meant all along.

So, next time you think:
"I've really let myself go."
To your strong birthing body,
Some kindness, please show.

MATERNITY KNICKERS

I wonder if I packed away
all my maternity knickers,
Would these stubborn paws of mine
stop reaching for the snickers?

Whether it be day or night,
I always have the munchies.
And life's too short to say goodbye
To all the twirls and crunchies!

BEAUTY

Stay true to yourself.
Shine your light near and far
For, in fact, you ARE beautiful
JUST are you are.

FRIENDSHIPS

Supporting and being
supported by those we love

A FRIEND LIKE YOU

There are some people in this life
Who make the world much brighter:
Who radiate warmth inside out,
And make us all feel lighter.

They pull us up when we feel low.
Their smiles can cure a lot.
And, often, they don't even know
The marvellous gift they've got.

So, if you know someone like this,
I urge you hold them close.
For, in the tough times that you'll face,
You'll long for them the most.

Remind them that you love them
And be there to help them too.
Be forever thankful for
The friend they've been to you.

I, for one, am blessed with
many people in my life
Who fit this bill, and walk with me,
In good times and in strife.

And so I pray this gift they have,
That I can share it too.
So I can be to one and all
A marvellous friend like you.

let the
wine of
friendship
never run
dry
alice
atkinson

THE STRUGGLE OF THE JUGGLE

I'm sorry if I cancel
Or say I cannot go.
I do not mean to disappoint.
I'm trying hard, you know.

I've eggs in many baskets
And I want to do it all.
I'm juggling and struggling.
I'm so afraid to fall.

I want to keep you happy
And all the others too,
But the truth is that I'm failing
To keep up with all of you.

I care so much and want to share
Your highs and lows and more,
But it's hard to be as present
As the friend I was before.

These little beings that we've made
Consume my energy.
And if I ever get a minute,
I crave some silence to just BE..

..Be alone and be at rest,
A luxury I rarely get,
And while I want to know what's happening,
I need to just forget

The jobs, the tasks, and all the roles
I daily have to play,
And to spend time with my littles
Who won't always be this way.

I'm surviving, never thriving.
My heads barely above water.
My priorities now need to be
my son and darling daughter.

So, again, I'm truly sorry
If I sometimes don't reply.
I love you dearly, never fear,
I'm just trying to get by.

THE BABIES BORN SLEEPING

This one's for all those mourning:
All the babies that have gone.
Tragic losses, ever cherished:
They must be reflected on.

"I've just had a baby,
But there's no baby in my arm?"
I'm numb with pain and filled with grief.
My baby's come to harm.

Be it near the start or further on,
Gestation does not matter.
For once we see those two straight lines,
We foresee that pitter patter

of tiny feet, and, just like that,
we plan our lives with them.
From conception, all our hopes and dreams
for their future do stem.

So, when a loved one loses
their adored, beloved baby,
Let them weep and sit with you.
Don't try to tell them: "Maybe

your body isn't ready yet", Or
"At least you weren't further gone",
For that does not offer solace
On the road they embark on.

Say: "I'm sorry" and "I love you"
And that they did nothing wrong.
Tell them you'll be there for them,
On this road, however long.

Do not minimise their loss.
Lend a non-judgemental ear.
For often, in this time of grief,
They'll just want to know you're here.

NIGHT-TIME SONGS

Those Lullabies at Slumber Time

THE WONDER OF YOU

Sometimes I watch you sleeping,
Heavy eyelids o'er your eyes,
And I wonder what you'll dream of,
As the darkness fills the skies.

I wonder if I'll feature
In the lands you'll venture to.
Happy places, worry free:
Please take me there with you.

I wonder when will be the last time
You call for me at night.
And when will be the last time
You hold my hand so tight.

When will be the last time
I fulfil your every need.
For all these times will someday end:
That is one thing guaranteed.

Then, finally, I wonder,
When those last times come and go,
What new adventures will await:
It's a joy to watch you grow.

A Love So Strong

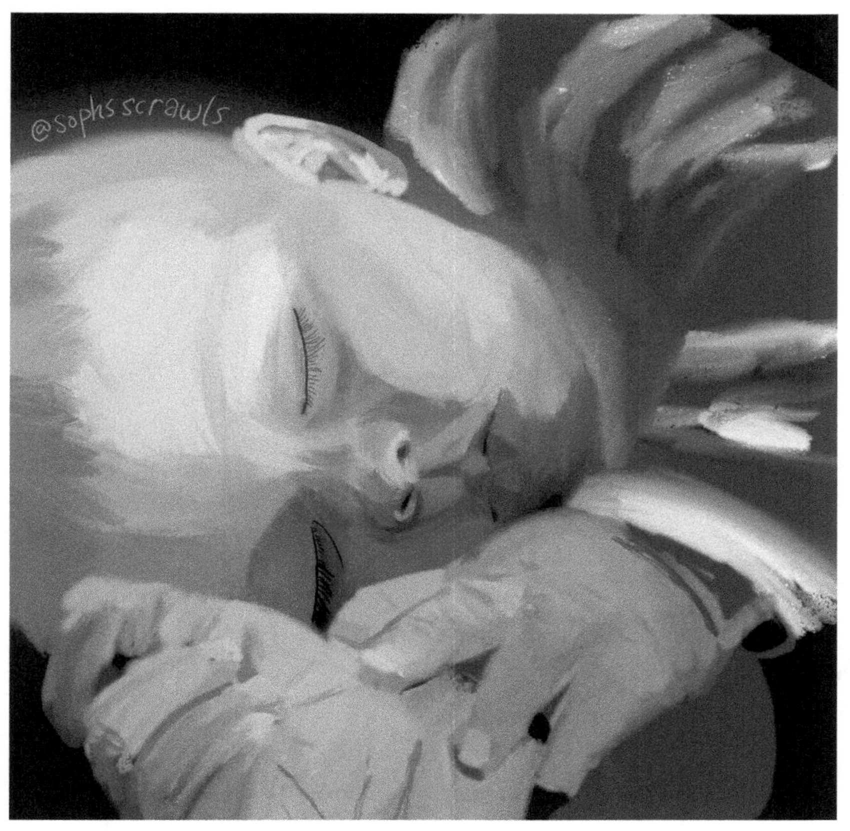

EXHALE

Sink into my arms at the end of the day.
Let mama chase all those worries away.
You are strong. You are brave.
You can ride any wave.
But, for now, fast asleep on my chest you will stay.

ROCK YOU TO SLEEP

Tonight in my arms
I did rock you to sleep.
And I was overcome
by a feeling so deep.

A wave of emotion
swept right over me,
and I hoped and I prayed
that I would always be:

Your safe place, your haven,
Your comfort and home.
The arms you return to
Where'er you might roam.

The solace you seek
when on hard times you fall.
The one that you turn to:
No worry's too small.

So, rest well, dear angel,
May your slumber be deep.
And as long as you need me,
I'll rock you to sleep.

A Love So Strong

MY HAPPY PLACE

As you succumbed to sleep tonight,
Nestled in, so near,
The last thing that you said to me
Was: "Mama, please stay here."

Your breath then slowed, your eyelids closed.
You cuddled into me.
In all the world, there is no place,
That I would rather be.

EACH DAY MY LOVE WILL GROW

"Just a little longer mum.
I don't want you to go."

"Never will I leave you dear:
Each day my love will grow."

STAY WITH ME

"Mama, won't you stay with me?
Please, Mama: stay right here.
Won't you sleep with me tonight.
I want you to be near.

The clothes can wait, there's plenty more,
And I don't care what's on the floor.

So, Mama, won't you stay me right here."

Maria Tempany @therhymingone

IT'S TIME TO SLEEP

It's time to sleep my little one.
The darkness floods the skies.
You've had a busy day today.
It's time to close those eyes.

Tomorrow is another day,
With lots of games for us to play.

In every day, a new adventure lies.

LINGER A LITTLE LONGER

Linger a little longer
As you lay them down tonight.
Cling a little closer
As the darkness steals the light.

They'll never be as little
As in this moment here.
Soothe a little softer
And hold them oh so near.

Let all the worries of the day
Float up to the skies.
Gaze a little deeper
Into those precious eyes.

Tell them that you love them,
That they're special and they're strong.
Linger a little longer
For they won't be little long.

About the Author

This is Maria Tempany's second book
of poetry on motherhood.
Maria is a medical doctor and lives in Dublin with her
husband, Joe, her 3-year-old son, Johnny,
and her 18-month-old daughter, Edie.
The art of poetry has been a much-treasured outlet for her
amidst the trying throes of early parenthood.
Her first book, 'A Mother's Birth',
has been an international success.
More of her poetry can be found under the alias of
@therhymingone on social media.

Lightning Source UK Ltd.
Milton Keynes UK
UKHW022015200922
409143UK00010B/2956